Praise for *You Have a Hammer*

"Informed and conversational, this little gem of a book tells it like it is... and how it should be. This is the thinking person's guide to reimagining the purpose of grant funding and how you can use it to achieve change. Floersch challenges everything you thought you knew about the world of grants, from how and why to seek them to their purpose and potential. She distills her decades of experience into this powerful little book to remind us that the best nonprofits work to achieve change and that securing grant funding is just one means to that end."

– Michael Renner, Strategist at
Missouri Foundation for Health

"Preparing grant proposals in an era of upheaval in the funding arena is somewhat bipolar. It has to be both precise and nuanced. In her book *You Have a Hammer: Building Grant Proposals for Social Change,* Floersch makes it clear this is an evolving society and changing the perception of the grantmaking process is going to take work. There are also some cornerstones of the practice that will outlive all of us. You don't often get this much direction in a short tome."

– Paul Clolery, Editor-in-Chief of
The NonProfit Times

"Raising money for social change is more important than ever in an era of extreme inequality, ecological crisis, and growing threats to democracy. But even the most passionate advocates won't find the funds needed to drive impact without first understanding grants as tools for pursuit of the common good. This book is a great place to start."

– David Callahan, Founder & Editor of
Inside Philanthropy and author of *The Givers*

"How often do you pick up a book on philanthropy and then simply can't put it down? This small book is pure gold and a must read for anyone engaged in grants development. Really quite brilliant in its simplicity and approach."

– Cynthia M. Adams, Founder & CEO
of GrantStation.com, Inc.

"Floersch suggests that we balance best-practice and innovation in our grantseeking, and that is exactly what she does here, with fine-tuned practical advice in the context of a powerful argument for grantseeking as a social change practice. The path to successful grant proposals offered here is integrity, including honest appraisals of ourselves and our work, and respectful consideration of funders and their mission. Walking the talk of respectful relationships and careful thinking is what leads to the 'righteous ask,' and only a righteous ask brings the sustained support we all seek. If you have anything to do with driving financial support for social change, whether just starting out or well into the life of your organization, I encourage you to read this book. Floersch's call to action has changed the way I talk about our work—and that change is already bearing fruit."

– Lucinda J. Garthwaite, Ed.D, Director of The Institute for Liberatory Innovation

"*You Have a Hammer* is a little book with a big heart and a lot of common sense. In the high-stress world of competitive funding, it's easy to chase opportunities and lose sight of what matters most—the people and communities who rely on the success of your work. This little book shares some of the critical lessons Floersch has shared with thousands of grantseekers around the US and internationally. I credit her teaching and mentorship with my success in securing millions of grant dollars and those lessons continue to inform my work as a grant maker. A real strength of this book is Floersch's engaging and authentic communications style. I'm so pleased she continues to share her knowledge to support your success in addressing critical social issues."

– Kevin Wiberg, Philanthropic Advisor for Community Engagement at the Vermont Community Foundation

"Floersch explains the real power of grant proposal writing as a tool for social change and as a way to deepen community collaboration. By following her approach, nonprofits can escape the fund-chasing model and stand to make real change."

– Kelly Thomas, Fund Development Consultant and former Director of Development of the Tiyya Foundation

"This book is an invaluable resource that reminds the grants profession of why our minds should be set on our work as a vehicle for social change. Based on her extensive experience, Floersch provides mini-chapters of important information for building effective grant proposals that result in lasting community impact. Get *You Have a Hammer: Building Grant Proposals for Social Change* and keep it close at hand as a reference and as an inspiration."

– Dr. Bernard Turner, GPC, Associate Professor of Social Entrepreneurship at Belmont University, member and past president of the Grant Professionals Association

"This book is such a gift to the grants profession. Floersch provides awesome, meaty, actionable, inspiring content in a concise manner, and her deep knowledge, experience, and passion for the grants profession come through on every page. *You Have a Hammer: Building Grant Proposals for Social Change* is a must read for all grant professionals. Knowing 'how' to write a grant request is helpful, but understanding the 'why' is something that can set your requests apart and increase your probability of success. I recommend this book to everyone just starting their journey – and also to those striving for constant improvement."

– Tammy Tilzey, Director of Foundant for Grantseekers at Foundant Technologies

"*You Have A Hammer* is an inspirational, motivational step-by-step field guide in how to ground our proposals in activism, vocation, and social justice. From understanding your agency's truth to strategizing how your proposal becomes an effective agent for change, *You Have A Hammer* is an invitation to join a movement of social equity. Floersch does a brilliant job of encouraging us to grow, pour passion into mission, confront bias, lead with integrity, and be willing to take reasonable risks. This book will reenergize you and reawaken your awareness that you are an instrumental part of the greater good in our world."

– Colleen Coffey, Executive Director of The College Planning Collaborative at Framingham State University and Mass Bay Community College

"Floersch's book is a quick and powerful primer for mission-driven leaders seeking an introduction to grant proposals. This is not your standard grantwriting book. *You Have a Hammer: Building Grant Proposals for Social Change* is an engaging and essential social change guide that will help you make your next righteous ask!"

– Morgan Webster, Director of
Common Good Vermont

"*You Have a Hammer: Building Grant Proposals for Social Change* is Floersch's latest contribution to the field of grantsmanship. In this easy-to-read book she affirms The Grantsmanship Center's philosophy of using grant proposals to develop, implement, and evaluate a plan for social transformation. *You Have a Hammer* is a 'why-to book' that urges you to start your organization's enlightened odyssey to use grants as one way to draft your community's blueprint for social change."

– Stephen D. Clark, community liaison and
advocate, and retired Senior Management
Analyst at the US Department of Housing and
Urban Development

"Rather than another how-to book on writing successful grant proposals, Floersch calls for a paradigm shift in our nonprofit field from supplicant to change agent, urging teamwork within our organizations and communities as well as equitable partnerships with funding agencies. Her clarion call is to focus on impact and change, not merely on activities."

– John Killacky, Vermont House of Representatives
legislator and former Executive Director of
Flynn Center for the Performing Arts

"Floersch has never been content to tread water: she swims upstream, determined to use grants as a tool for addressing the root issues of human needs. *You Have a Hammer* is the kind of book that gets better and better with each reading."

– Charles R. Putney, External Consultant for
Higher Education at McAllister & Quinn, Inc.

You Have a Hammer

You Have a Hammer

Building Grant Proposals for Social Change

By Barbara Floersch

Foreword by Aaron Dorfman
President & CEO, National Committee for Responsive Philanthropy

First Printing: January 26, 2021

You Have a Hammer: Building Grant Proposals for Social Change

ISBN: 978-1-57869-045-9
Library of Congress Control Number: 2020915441

Published by Rootstock Publishing an imprint of Multicultural Media, Inc.
www.rootstockpublishing.com
info@rootstockpublishing.com

Art and Book Design: Mason Singer, Laughing Bear Associates
Cover illustration: Bonnie Acker
Author photo: Larry Floersch

Printed in the USA

Dedicated to Dorothy Watson Smith
and Josephine Koen Smith

Contents

Through philanthropy, people can address aspects of the common good that have been overlooked or neglected by government.

Foreword

How do we pursue the common good in society? Government certainly plays a vitally important role. Through taxation, spending, and setting the rules by which society operates, government done right ensures the most good for the most people.

Philanthropy is another way we pursue the common good. It's never a substitute for government, but it does play an important complementary role. Through philanthropy, people can address aspects of the common good that have been overlooked or neglected by government.

At its best, philanthropy is a partnership between donors and the nonprofits they fund to make change. Donors and foundations can't make the world better on their own. They need nonprofits that deliver services, advocate for better public policies, and improve lives in countless ways. Nonprofits can't do all the amazing work they do on their own, either. They need funding from grantmakers and other donors to make an impact.

In this excellent short book, Barbara Floersch helps those who write grant proposals think about their work in new ways. She helps us see ourselves as applicants, not supplicants. She helps us understand that we're not grubbing for dollars but rather seeking true partners for the work. She helps us think about how to invite potential donors to join us in working on important causes.

While this is definitely not a "how-to" book, I'm certain that those who read it and truly internalize Barbara's advice will dramatically increase the revenue they bring to their organizations and to the issues they care about most.

Early in my career, I led two different small grassroots nonprofit organizations with budgets under $500,000. Raising money was always a challenge. I wish this book had been available to me then. It would have made me a better champion for the organizations I was leading and the important causes we advocated.

– Aaron Dorfman
President & CEO, National Committee for Responsive Philanthropy

The dollars you bring in
light fires that keep burning.
The very process of the work
builds and empowers
the community.

Introduction

There are currently hundreds of how-to books about developing grant proposals—how to tell a better story, how to grab the funder's attention, how to do it if you're a dummy or a genius, how to jump to the front of the line and bring in the dollars.

But even now, in 2020, Norton Kiritz's 1980 how-to publication, *Program Planning & Proposal Writing*, remains the seminal work in the field. It established the model that those seeking grants still use to develop proposals and that funders still use to develop application guidelines. It was named "the grantseekers' Bible" by the *New York Times* in 2006, has been used in over 40 countries by over a million people, and has been published in four languages.

In 2015, The Grantsmanship Center, which was founded by Kiritz, published an updated and expanded edition of that work, which I was honored to author. The new edition, *Grantsmanship: Program Planning & Proposal Writing*, resonates with Kiritz's thundering voice, fierce integrity, and egalitarian philosophy. Like the original, it isn't about grabbing dollars. It's about grants as tools for social change.

I was mentored by Kiritz, who died in 2006, but I've also been schooled by my own experience in raising millions of grant dollars, reviewing hundreds of grant proposals, and teaching thousands of nonprofit staff members about grantsmanship. This book is my contribution to the field. My greatest hope is that it complements Kiritz's seminal work.

If you want to bring in grant dollars, you have to understand the how-to of the work. But if you fail to understand the essence of the work, the dollars in your pocket won't amount to much when it comes to impact. Continue to refine your skills: the world needs intelligent, competent grants professionals. But don't rush to bring in grant funding until you're well grounded in what you're fighting for.

When you do this work right, you're both a rainmaker and a changemaker, and the grant proposal is a tool you wield in pursuit of social transformation. The dollars you bring in light fires that keep burning. The very process of developing grant proposals helps build and empower the community.

This book is about the essence of grantsmanship. It's about the philosophy and viewpoint essential to honest, changemaking work. This is not a how-to book. It's a why-to book and that's where you need to start.

– Barbara Floersch

1

You're Not a Grantwriter

To continue to move the field forward, let's make sure our professional language evolves along with our skills and understanding. You do not *write grants.* Really, you don't. It's an old notion that was never right in the first place.

A grant is the funding awarded to an organization by a grantmaker. Grantmakers award (write) grants. Organizations seeking grant funding don't write grants, they write *grant proposals, funding applications, requests for funding,* and the like.

If you're doing the work right, you're doing much more than writing.

This is not about semantics. It's more important than that. Consistently and consciously referring to funding requests as proposals begins changing how you view the whole process. If you're one of the thousands of people addicted to the terms *grantwriting* and *grantwriter,* just give this a try. Enforce a self-imposed moratorium on using those terms for a couple of months and then reflect on the work you've been doing. I think you'll find that neither term is a good fit.

Here's why. When you produce grant proposals, you do much more than stare at a computer screen and click-clack away writing documents meant to bring in money. You do the research, get the facts, line up the players, and pull together a team to make a plan. Then you produce funding requests to fuel the activities required to make change happen.

Of course, you have to be a competent writer to articulate the situation and the plan, but the writing part of proposal development is only a small piece of the entire effort. It's time to move on from the term *grantwriting*. If you're doing the work right, you're doing much more than writing. And even if you're only doing the writing, you're not writing grants.

Since the term *grantwriting* is inaccurate and doesn't capture the depth and breadth of your work, try moving on to terms such as *grant proposal development, proposal development,* or *proposal writing*. Since *grantwriter* isn't the right title, how about *grants specialist, community development specialist, community organizer, chief of proposal development, changemaker*, or *partnership specialist?* You decide. I'll wager you can come up with lots of titles that accurately reflect your role.

Original version published in The Grantsmanship Center Blog (2016).
Updated version published in the *NonProfit Times* (2018).
Material used with permission of The Grantsmanship Center.

4

What Is a Grant Proposal?

A grant proposal is more than a request for money. Money, of course, is involved in the transaction, but that's not what the transaction is really about.

Your organization exists for the purpose defined in its mission statement. Whether you're working to ensure public access to high-quality art or to end poverty, the integrity and value of your organization depends on its faithfulness to that purpose. A grant proposal is one of the tools you use to fuel your drive toward the mission. It's many other things as well.

A grant proposal is a tool for building partnerships and a blueprint for change.

A grant proposal is an invitation into a partnership. It asks the funder to join your team in accomplishing something important. Your organization has the multilayered community connections and on-the-ground muscle needed to make things happen. The funder has the resources to fuel the work and the connections to help sustain it. When you submit a grant proposal, you aren't asking for a handout, you're asking for a handshake.

A grant proposal is a specific kind of advocacy. By developing and submitting a grant proposal, you're taking a high-profile stand on an issue and waving a flag to rally assistance and energy. You do the community organizing and collaboration that are required to bring people together and incite action, and when the proposal is righteous, a rejection of your grant request doesn't stop the momentum. Committed organizations stay the course, make the case, talk it up, and continue to reach out until the necessary pieces, including funding, are in place.

A grant proposal is a participatory research report. To wrestle down a problem and figure out how to solve it, you've got to dive deep into the facts and figures of the situation, read about what others are doing, and study approaches that have been effective. You have to engage in discussion and debate with other nonprofits, community groups, and those affected by the situation. Research and debate help sort out the pieces, deepen the conversation, expose the nuances, and make sure you're on track.

Most of all, a grant proposal is an argument for change. It describes a problem that needs to be tackled, or an opportunity that should be seized, and makes a case for taking action. It explains the urgency, lays out a plan, and specifies the intended results of the work.

A grant proposal is many other things as well. It's a blueprint for your work—a set of instructions. It articulates the understandings of all who are involved —it's an agreement. It lays out specific expectations for change—it's a yardstick against which you'll measure success. It details income and costs—it's a financial plan.

Thinking of a grant proposal strictly as a funding request diminishes much of its changemaking potential and devalues your role. To embrace the power of your work, step beyond the limited, traditional definition.

What Is a Grant Award?

In the most basic sense, a grant award is the money a funder gives an organization in response to a grant proposal. But if you limit yourself to that definition, you'll limit your effectiveness as a social activist and will be less successful in winning grants. Money is involved in the transaction, but again, that's not what the transaction is really about.

A grant award is a social investment and a wager that your organization can deliver results.

Each funder has a mission —a purpose that motivates and defines its work. And just like other nonprofits, different funders focus on different issues. But as diverse as they are, grantmakers have one thing in common. They use grants as tools to accomplish their mission.

Grant funding fuels the action, and nonprofits use that fuel to get the job done. Nonprofits are the vehicles through which funders work, and the grant proposal and award process is one way funders identify robust, capable nonprofits with which to partner.

Thinking of grant awards in this way brings two issues into sharp focus:

First, to win grants your organization's mission and the project for which you're seeking support must be a spot-on fit with the funder to which you're applying. Only thorough research can tell you which funders have missions and interests compatible with yours. A general search on the internet won't do. You must educate yourself about the considerations and nuances that define a good-fit funder and use a professional-level database designed specifically for funder research. Finding the grantmakers most likely to support your work takes significant time, but that time is a necessary investment.

Second, the capacity and credibility of your organization are paramount. When you've submitted a compelling grant request to just the right funder for just the right project, it's the credibility of your organization that will seal or kill the deal. You won't win an award unless the funder believes you can deliver what you promise. Demonstrating strong leadership, a mission-driven approach, appropriate expertise, a record of accomplishment, a history of collaboration, and financial stability is just as important as a solid plan for tackling an issue of mutual concern. Everyone can talk, but not everyone can accomplish. Funders are looking for organizations that can take the project to the finish line.

A grant award to your organization is an investment in the funder's own mission. It's also an expression of confidence in your organization's effectiveness and a wager that you can deliver results.

Know Your Field

To plan a good program and make a convincing case for funding, you have to know what you're talking about. Without a solid grounding in your field, it's easy to recreate wheels, propose approaches that have proved to be futile, and show up at the back of the curve instead of on the cutting edge.

To do good work you've got to know what you're talking about.

You don't need to be a take-it-to-the-mat subject matter expert to develop proposals, but you do need an understanding of current theories, data, and discussions. You also need some understanding of the past, where the field has been and how it has moved forward. To be effective, you need to understand where the backwaters and the frontiers are.

Think of this as self-education, professional development, or simply preparation for the job. Your goal is to become well informed and to stay current.

You'll have to set your own course—there's no roadmap for this process. Give it thought, then dig in. Talk to experts and ask them what to read, what data sources to examine, and who else you should talk to. Visit the websites of government agencies, think tanks, and national organizations to find bibliographies, evaluation reports, the names of experts, and the names of respected publications. Explore academic journals. Join state and national associations to connect with others in the field and tune in to current conversations.

Your understanding of issues from a national and state perspective will provide context, help you interpret what's happening locally, and give you credibility. But focus on your home turf. A deep understanding of what's happening locally counts most.

Know Your Organization

When applying for grant funding, you need to understand the organization you represent. The organization's quality will be a big factor in your success, and the personalities, systems, and culture within the organization will affect your ability to do good work.

Before asking for grants, be sure you know what you represent.

Learn all you can about the services your organization provides. Identify the strengths you can build on and the challenges you'll have to overcome. Each organization presents its own range of complications, but here are a few questions to get you started.

Can you describe your organization in detail? You may need to interview staff members, review reports and evaluation studies, read grant proposals that fund some of the work your organization is doing, look at tax returns and budget reports, and talk with volunteers and clients. When you're done, you'll have a solid understanding of the organization's mission and structure, the nature of its services, the numbers of people it helps, its budget, and other key information. Hopefully, you'll be inspired and convinced that the organization is worth the blood, sweat, and tears you'll invest in raising grant dollars to support its work.

Do your administrators understand and practice grantsmanship? Many grants professionals are simply instructed to get more grants. That's it—no direction in terms of purpose or priority; no discussion of mission or partnerships. If that describes your boss, you have a problem. Do administrators in your organization understand the proper role of grants? Are they keyed in to the principles of grantsmanship or will you need to explain them and build their commitment to that philosophy?

Does your organization follow through on its commitments? A brilliant idea is worthless unless the team standing behind it has the will and capacity to turn that idea into reality. Does your organization stand behind important projects and stay the course? Is your group seen as a force for good that gets things done? Or does it cut and run when there's no money involved? When the organization has a solid reputation for follow-through, you'll find it much easier to line up community support and partnerships for grant proposals.

Is there a culture of teamwork? The best program plans and grant proposals are the result of teamwork. Do staff members understand their role in seeking grants and participate energetically? Or do they balk at the extra work and complain that it's your job, not theirs? You may need to help staff members understand why their input is critical and why it serves their best interests.

Are staff members on top of the latest developments in the field? In the best circumstances you'll have in-house experts who are enthusiastic about cutting-edge work, welcome the chance to innovate, and bring essential knowledge into program planning. In the worst circumstances you'll have staff members who have given up inquiry, resist change, and are invested in maintaining the status quo because it's comfortable. Usually you'll find a range of attitudes presenting best- to worst-case scenarios. You need to know who you have to work with, who can and will help you, and when you'll need to seek outside assistance.

Is there evidence that your programs and services are effective? Maybe your organization is data savvy and you'll find a rich vein of well-digested data you can mine. Or maybe your organization gathers a large amount of data but doesn't analyze or use it. In the worst circumstances, you'll find that data gathering and analysis are neglected altogether. When you know what's available, you can use it, and when you know what's missing, you can advocate for gathering new information and establishing new reporting systems. Data matter. You can't do good work without it.

No organization is perfect. You can't expect that. But you can expect an environment that promotes integrity and professionalism. You need confidence that the organization's work is worth the investment of your effort.

It's Never About Your Organization

A nonprofit organization is only important because of the benefits it brings to the community. It's only valuable because of the difference it makes in the lives of those it serves. Funders do not make grants to keep programs running or to ensure that staff members keep their jobs. They make grants to produce positive results in communities, and through that, to fulfill their own social missions.

Focus every grant proposal on those who will benefit.

Most people who work for nonprofits are committed to their organization. They take pride in the good work it produces and feel rewarded well beyond the often-meager salary they receive for work weeks that often stretch beyond 40 hours. But when they're developing grant proposals, that fierce commitment is easily communicated in a way that tilts the argument for support in the wrong direction.

For example, suppose the elder daycare center has lost a chunk of funding and, without new resources, will be forced to cut back services. In a sincere plea for grant support, staff members are likely to warn that without new funding the program will be scaled back by 50 percent and five staff members will lose their jobs.

Unfortunately, this all-too-typical argument is pointed in the wrong direction. It focuses on the organization and its staff rather than on the people served. If services are cut back, how many elderly people and families will be affected? What will happen to those who count on the program? How will the cutback affect the community?

One way to thwart organization-focused grant requests is to be sure every single proposal explains how the situation you want to address affects those you serve. In what way does it cause or threaten harm? Or in what way is it a meaningful opportunity for improvement? Be specific.

Also explain how those you serve will benefit if the grant request is funded. Will lives be improved, rivers be cleaner, or animals be rescued? Provide details.

An organization-focused grant request assumes funders understand the results produced by the applicant's programs. That assumption is incorrect. Every request for grant funding is a call to action that must explain why the situation to be addressed is significant to those the organization serves and how addressing the situation will provide meaningful benefits.

To drive the point home, let's review several types of grant requests.

- The purpose of a *general operating grant* is not to keep the doors open and ensure that staff members keep their jobs. It's to ensure that the organization can continue to deliver benefits to the community. The argument will be based on the results the organization produces, and those results will be documented.

- The purpose of a grant to strengthen the organization's infrastructure is not to update a database. It's to enable the organization to serve its beneficiaries more effectively. The proposal will explain how the current outdated technology decreases efficiency and how upgraded information technology will contribute to more effective programming or efficiencies that will improve services to clients.

- The purpose of a grant to start a new program isn't to offer exciting activities. It's to improve the quality of life in the community by confronting a problem or seizing an opportunity. The proposal will show that the issue is significant to those the organization serves and explain the specific, measurable results the program will produce.

- The purpose of a grant to expand service capacity is not to wipe out your organization's addiction treatment waiting list. It's to aid people who desperately need it.

The proposal will document the hardship that delays in service cause those awaiting treatment and will explain the specific, measurable results service expansion will produce for beneficiaries.

- The purpose of a grant to sustain a program through a funding cut is not to maintain the program and ensure staff members keep their jobs. It's to ensure that people who depend on the services do not suffer hardship or harm while other, longer-term funding strategies are put into place. The proposal will document the benefits people receive from the program, explain the hardships a cutback would cause them, and describe long-range plans for securing program services.

Every dollar you raise from whatever source is simply a tool to help your organization accomplish its mission. Focus every grant proposal you prepare on those who benefit from your organization's work, not on your organization.

Don't Grab for Grants

Seeking grants is typically approached in one of two ways. In the first approach, the nonprofit comes across a funding opportunity and goes in search of a project it can shoehorn into the application guidelines. In the second approach, the nonprofit identifies a funding need and goes in search of a funder. Both approaches are reactive—the opposite of proactive and strategic.

Build partnerships with funders. Be proactive. Exchange ideas. Get to know each other. Make a *righteous ask.*

In the first approach, dreaming up projects in response to a grant opportunity is, clearly and simply, chasing dollars. Avoid the temptation. Instead, assess how opportunities align with your organization's strategic plan, support its mission, and relate to documented community needs. If you can check the right boxes, go for it. If not, walk away.

The flaw in the second approach is less obvious, but when you compare the task of identifying grant funders to the task of identifying major individual donors, the drawback becomes clearer.

Experienced fundraisers who secure major gifts from individual donors don't wait until there's an urgent funding need before researching and nurturing relationships that may lead to contributions. Their job is to establish a pipeline of donations to support their organization's work. To build that pipeline, they constantly prospect. They comb through their organization's records, talk with board members and other friends, read the local news, and use every means available to identify the people who are most likely to make substantial contributions. It's about research, nurturing relationships, timing, and finally asking for a donation in the way that is best suited to each potential donor.

Approaching grant funding the same way has huge advantages. When you do the research to identify the foundations and corporations that are a good fit with your organization's work, you end up with a solid understanding of the players in the field and know who to reach out to.

The idea is to build partnerships with funders, exchange ideas, and get to know each other. Then, when a need comes up that's an exact fit with one of your funding partners, you can make a *righteous ask.* A *righteous ask* is a funding request grounded in a community need that is well aligned with the funder's mission and put forth by a well-respected nonprofit in pursuit of impact rather than dollars. When you work this way, your organization is much more likely to receive the support it requests.

A *righteous* ask is grounded in a community need, aligned with a funder's mission, and seeks impact rather than dollars.

The same applies to government funding. When you've identified government grant programs that are well aligned with your organization's work, you can move strategically. You can study programs funded in past competitions, look at winning proposals, line up plans and partners, and begin gathering supportive data.

We all know that government funding is volatile. It's subject to the ebb and flow of public opinion, world events, and politics. Staying informed of current local and national issues will give you a heads-up about funding opportunities that are likely to emerge. Concern over school shootings led to grant programs to enhance school safety. After 9/11, many federal grant programs pivoted toward emergency preparedness and homeland security. The 2020 pandemic spurred public health funding and is likely to result in grants to shore up employment and economic development. The 2020 uprising for racial justice is the catalyst for numerous foundation grant opportunities, and at the federal level may result in grants for training police officers and developing new approaches to improve community safety.

Being educated about existing government grant programs and emerging social issues means you'll be less subject to the wild, last-minute responses to just-released guidelines that often lead to poorly planned programs, mistakes, and burnout.

When you assess current events within the context of grant funding, you can begin gathering data, building partnerships, and planning programs well before grant programs are finalized and roll into competition.

Grant opportunity alert services, which are offered by various companies and by grants.gov for federal competitions, can tip you off to fast-breaking opportunities. But use these services only to supplement your own research. They can't replace the deep digging and exploration that will uncover your most likely funding partners. Using alert services alone can too easily propel you into a grabbing frenzy: Here's one! There's one! Which shall I choose? How many can I submit? If you take that approach, before long you will have lost any notion of purpose other than snatching dollars.

To do it right, the initial research will take a substantial amount of time. That's a challenge. Maybe you can find an intern to help, seclude yourself for a deep dive, or peck away at it bit by bit. After your initial effort, you'll also have to keep it current.

Most importantly, use the research. The valuable information you'll have in hand will be worthless unless you do something with it. Work with others in your organization to develop a plan of action. How can you best reach out to the strongest prospects? Who might be able to offer introductions? Which grantmakers are best suited for which programs?

Line up funding needs with the list of prospects and establish a schedule for developing and submitting proposals. A thorough, steady, well-considered approach to funder research and relationship-building is well worth the investment of resources and energy.

"You're an Applicant, Not a Supplicant"

– Norton Kiritz, *Program Planning & Proposal Writing,* The Grantsmanship Center, 1980.

Both grantmakers and nonprofit organizations unwittingly perpetuate the stereotype of grant-seekers as beggars. With such a huge power imbalance between those who ask and those who give, it's easy to understand why the image persists. But to accomplish our best work, we need to move beyond it.

Grantmakers and grantseekers are a team! Authentic partnerships get the best results.

Grantmakers and nonprofits need each other. Funders need the expertise, community access, and muscle of nonprofits. Non-profits need grantmakers' resources as well as their honest, transparent partnership. Grantmakers and grantseekers are a team, and only when we build authentic, mutually respectful partnerships will the work we accomplish together rise to be the best that is possible.

To change the beggar/benefactor dynamic, both grantmakers and grantseekers have work to do. There's responsibility on both sides.

The sad fact is that many nonprofits are guilty of chasing dollars. Faced with an urgent and continuous need for cash, seeking grants easily devolves into a money-grabbing frenzy. I have met thousands of nonprofit staff members who are instructed by administrators to shake every tree that could possibly throw out a grant dollar.

Organizations that chase dollars see a funding opportunity, think up some project to shoehorn into a proposal, and then run after the grant. On the other hand, organizations that practice grantsmanship see issues that need to be tackled, work with those affected, build partnerships with like-minded organizations, and make plans. Eventually, if required, they look for money to support the work. They don't respond to funding opportunities, they respond to community needs.

That proactive, community-building approach encourages authentic partnerships with funders and builds mutual respect.

The first step in breaking the dollar-chasing addiction is to make sure board members and administrators understand what grantsmanship is and the righteous function of grant funding within an organization. That understanding will dissuade them from demanding that staff members "just get a grant—any grant—right now!"

The second step is to get serious about building a variety of funding streams. Even modest individual giving and annual membership programs that can be grown over time will pay great dividends in the long run.

To work in true partnership with funders, grant-seekers must also claim their power. Non-profits are formidable engines for social change with multilayered community connections and deep on-the-ground know-how. Norton Kiritz admonished grantseekers to stand tall when he thundered, "You're applicants, not supplicants. Don't beg." When you submit a grant proposal, you're offering funders an opportunity to participate in meaningful, changemaking work.

Advocating for ourselves as grantseekers is crucial because so long as grantmakers continue to eschew full-cost funding, general operating support, infrastructure upgrades, and multiyear grants, the nonprofit sector will suffer. Be sure your voice is well informed and well reasoned, and also be sure it's loud enough to be heard.

Take and make opportunities to communicate with funders about what you know and what you think. The experiences of nonprofits and the people they serve provide a perspective that is essential for figuring out the best approaches for addressing the myriad issues confronting our communities. You and your beneficiaries have something important to say and a fundamental role to play in social change.

Equitable partnerships between funders and grantees will move everyone's mission forward.

A Grant Is Not the Solution to Every Funding Need

Grants are better suited to some purposes than others, and just because your organization needs money doesn't necessarily mean it needs a grant.

Fundraising professionals focus on individual giving, membership drives, product sales, events, and other renewable income streams that can be used flexibly and grown over time. Done right, this sort of fund development can be the goose that lays the golden eggs that keep coming.

Don't try to shoehorn every funding need into a grant proposal.

Grant funding, on the other hand, is less flexible and less renewable than other forms of fundraising. Grants are usually earmarked for a specific purpose articulated in a grant proposal, and most funders limit grants to a few years. It's short-term support. Some grantmakers renew awards for longer periods, but as Norton Kiritz said in *Program Planning & Proposal Writing*, "Few want to adopt a program as a long-term dependent."

In general, grants are best suited for producing change that will be self-perpetuating over time, for testing new approaches, for accomplishing work that will be completed in a set time frame, for starting up new services that can be maintained by other funding streams, for strengthening internal systems to ensure continued organizational impact, or for addressing immediate crisis-level issues that can't wait for more long-term fundraising plans to mature.

When a grant-funded program results in policies or laws that change education, health care, justice, or other systems for the better, you can expect the results to be self-perpetuating without the need for substantial, ongoing cash investments. When a program demonstrates a new, successful approach for tackling a persistent problem, that approach can be shared broadly with others and institutionalized within existing systems.

A Grant Is Not the Solution to Every Funding Need

Grants are a great resource for starting new programs to address unmet needs. But take care. Funders want to know that their investment will pay off in the long term. That means a plan for sustaining impact beyond the period of grant funding will be a major deciding factor in whether you win an award.

Some funders award grants to support ongoing costs such as salaries, facility expenses, legal fees, and audits. But trying to support general operations by jumping from grant to grant is not a viable strategy. Focus on supporting general operations with sustainable income streams that can be expanded over time and use grants as a supplement.

Suppose you need to add a new staff position. If you win a grant to put that position in place, how will you sustain it once the grant runs out?

Suppose you need $1,000 worth of paper products for a homeless shelter. Is a grant request the most reasonable approach? Wouldn't requesting donations from local retailers be more sensible?

Before jumping to the conclusion that your organization needs a grant, ask a few questions.

1) Is it likely you can get someone to donate what you need instead?

2) Is the value of the resource significant enough to justify the effort associated with identifying the correct funder, preparing a proposal, waiting for a response, and then handling reporting requirements if you win an award?

3) Will the grant be a good investment for the funder? Will it result in concrete, measurable changes that will move the funder's mission forward?

4) Will the grant produce benefits your organization can sustain beyond the period of funding?

When an organization is overly dependent on grants, the constant ebb and flow of dollars results in a stressed staff, fractured services, and the inability to approach its mission strategically. Organizations with varied, sustainable funding streams are stronger, more resilient, and have more impact. Don't try to shoehorn every funding need into a grant proposal.

Planning Programs

Your job description may be about finding funders and submitting proposals, but you'll often find yourself planning programs as well. That may seem illogical. You were hired to bring in grant money, not to be a subject-matter expert. But because you know how to work with funders and interpret application guidelines, it makes sense for you to be involved in planning. The role you play will depend on your skill set and your organization's understanding of grantsmanship.

Be deeply engaged in the planning process. Don't make unilateral decisions or dictate how services will be delivered.

Administrators who are savvy about grants understand the obligations that come along with the money. They understand that grant proposals must be aligned with organizational priorities because grant funding steers the organization in a particular direction. These administrators are likely to ensure that your involvement in planning is appropriate.

If you're well connected in the community, administrators may ask you to help them engage experts and partner organizations in the planning process. And if you're a good facilitator, they may ask you to guide the team to plan an approach to meet both community needs and funder requirements. Even if your skills are tightly limited to writing and submitting proposals, they'll want you involved to ensure the plan doesn't stray from the fundable path and gives you what you need to do your part.

But sometimes administrators won't have time for planning new programs and will pass that ball to you. When this happens, keep in mind that being responsible for a task does not mean you have to accomplish it alone. Pull together a team. Get input from clients, knowledgeable staff members, concerned community partners, and other experts. But also keep administrators briefed so they will be fully supportive of the finished product and can make course corrections if needed. This is no time for jack-in-the-box surprises.

If administrators don't understand the role of grants, you have a problem. They're likely to throw you a set of application guidelines and simply say "catch." If you ask how you're supposed to respond to those guidelines, they might say it's your job to figure that out—that you need to think something up. If you ask to meet with them to discuss options or brief them on your thinking, they might say they don't have time. If you tell them you're going to pull together a team, they might tell you to do your own job—not to push the work off on others. They might not realize that by doing this, they're instructing you to determine the course of the organization. If you dream up a program, submit a proposal, and win a grant, the organization is obligated to follow through—to deliver on whatever you came up with.

When administrators don't understand grantsmanship, educate them. Enlighten them about the role of grant funding and remind them that grant funding can steer the organization's course. It's appropriate for you to be deeply engaged in the planning process. It's not appropriate for you to make unilateral decisions about new services the organization will offer or dictate the manner in which services will be delivered. Even if it feels powerful, it's not right. Even if it succeeds for a while, it will eventually result in turmoil, with administrators and staff rebelling against your constructs.

Enjoy your role in program planning. It can be deeply rewarding. Just be sure the role is appropriate, because once a grant request is funded, your organization will be obliged to implement the plan.

Cultural Relevance

The role you'll play in planning programs will depend on your skill set and job description. But whether you lead the team or contribute as a team member, keeping cultural relevance front and center will result in more effective programs.

Involve the people and communities you serve in planning and operating your programs.

The cultural diversity within communities is immense, with diversity of race, language, religious beliefs, educational levels, sexual orientation and gender identification, country of origin, physical abilities, income levels, age, and more. Some groups view the world through a lens of life experiences such as trauma, illness, and abuse. Some groups have been historically marginalized, underrepresented, and underserved. Some are especially hard to reach or difficult to serve.

To ensure relevant programs, work with community members as partners in change. Invite them to the decision-making table. Ask questions and truly listen. The starting point is recognizing that the people your organization serves know more about their own problems and needs than anyone else.

Even if the diversity of the community is reflected in your organization's staff and on its board of directors, it is best to engage those beyond the organization's walls. Diverse organizations can still become insular and slide slowly into a "we know best" attitude.

Culturally relevant programs value diversity and ensure that activities, procedures, systems, and staffing are aligned to support the highest level of engagement and best outcomes for those who will participate. Here are some baseline considerations:

Confront your own bias. Everyone seems to be saddled with some unconscious bias, and before you can promote cultural relevance you have to confront and resolve your own bias. This is hard, messy work, and organizations often reach out to well-qualified consultants to help. Self-knowledge is an important step in building a culturally competent organization that offers culturally relevant services.

Consider systems. Institutional bias is a well-known problem, and even when an organization means well, some of its approaches may be discouraging or hurtful to the people it intends to help. A program registration process may include questions that seem standard to one person but that are offensive to someone from a different culture. A feedback form might be inaccessible to some unless it's produced in a different language or available in a different way for those who can't read.

Include beneficiaries. When those intended to benefit from a program help plan it, there is a higher likelihood that the program will succeed. Including them requires that you sidestep your own assumptions and focus on the reality of their experiences and on approaches they think will be most helpful.

Depending on your work, including beneficiaries in providing services can also strengthen the program. Their participation can make others in the group more comfortable and can provide you with an ongoing reality check on which activities are going well and which activities need adjustments.

Define the target population. Identifying the specific population you will assist is a primary step in program planning and essential to developing culturally relevant services. If you've only identified a broad group (e.g., teenagers), you will need to look deeper into its cultural composition. When a program will serve several groups, include program approaches to accommodate each group appropriately.

Recognize individuality. Remember, all people are unique individuals, not just stereotypical representations of their cultural group. Be sure the program plan recognizes and honors the culture of the group, but also treats people as individuals. Don't let the program cross the line into cultural stereotyping.

Educate yourself. A quick search on the internet for "publications on cultural competence" or on "cultural relevance" will yield all sorts of free, up-to-date material. The United States Substance Abuse and Mental Health Services Administration (samhsa.gov) offers several publications on cultural competence in treatment. Advocates for Youth (advocatesforyouth.org) offers various tips for creating culturally competent programs. With a little digging, you should be able to find materials specific to the type of services your organization provides.

Make sure the grant proposal you submit reflects your commitment to cultural relevance. Even if the application guidelines don't ask that specific question, demonstrate your commitment through the language you use, the program and evaluation plans, and inclusion of beneficiaries. Make it clear that your organization understands, honors, and involves the people and communities it serves.

A commitment to culturally relevant programs is a commitment to effectiveness.

Collaborate

Almost every nonprofit undertaking can be enhanced by partnering with others within the community. Fortunately, collaboration is now accepted by grantseekers and funders alike as a fundamental element of good program planning and implementation. Unfortunately, there are some nonprofits that continue to treat it only as a funder mandate and fail to embrace it as the powerful and necessary tool it is.

Collaboration is essential for social change.

To collaborate is to involve beneficiaries and other organizations, groups, and individuals in examining problems and figuring out solutions. Genuine collaboration is engagement, not just show. It requires listening and negotiation, not dictating.

It often results in programs that are operated jointly by various organizations, and it often means sharing grant funds.

When nonprofits eschew genuine collaboration, it is usually for one of two reasons. First, there's not yet an antidote for the corrupting nature of power. Even leaders of small nonprofits can become so captivated by their authority that they derail endeavors that would require them to share decision-making or money. They talk the talk required by funders, but they don't walk the walk.

Second, many nonprofit staff members don't fully understand collaboration or grasp its necessity. Real community impact isn't accomplished in isolation, outside the give-and-take discussion and shared action that characterize community life. When you are serious about tackling a problem, you have to harness the best of every available resource and apply every bit of intelligence and strength to get the job done. That's what collaboration is about.

The starting place for collaboration is always with those who are affected by a problem and whom your organization wishes to assist. Their insights and experiences are essential for defining the situation and figuring out which solutions are most likely to work. Even now, it is common to see grant proposals aimed at assisting the poor, the young, the elderly, the ill—with no evidence of their voices in the planning process. It's the familiar "do it to them" rather than "do it with them" mistake. The intended beneficiary has a right to be involved in the process. Beyond the moral imperative of respecting those you serve, when you involve them, you are much more likely to accomplish something significant—something that matters and that will last.

Next, look for others in the community who are concerned about the situation that's driving your organization to act. There will be private and public nonprofits with missions that include the issue, or intersect with it, and that have unique services, resources, or perspectives to offer. Businesses and institutions of higher education can also contribute significant assistance and knowledge.

To pull together a collaborative process of program planning, proposal writing, and program implementation, you'll have to facilitate discussions so that all voices are heard and honored. You'll have to maintain order and civility while ensuring that the hard decisions get made on time.

Genuine collaboration can be easy, but is more often difficult. You'll have to contend with disagreements. You'll have to make compromises that test your resolve. You'll have to sniff out those whose only true interest is getting a piece of the grant-funding pie.

But genuine collaboration is also uplifting. You'll be inspired by people working honestly and tirelessly to improve the community and to assist those in need. You'll be encouraged by compromises made in service of the greater good. You'll make lasting friendships, both personally and professionally.

At the end of the day, if you've done it right, you'll have a small battalion of colleague organizations and individuals lined up by your side and ready to help accomplish the work you could never accomplish alone.

Argue for Change, Not Activities

A grant proposal must convince a funder that the situation you plan to address is significant, that the changes (a.k.a. outcomes, results) you plan to achieve are meaningful, and that the methods you will use to produce results can get the job done. Think of the proposal as an attorney making your case in court. To win, the argument must be logical, thorough, and supported by evidence.

Funders must understand the problem and believe the activity can improve the situation.

When it comes to making a convincing case for funding, the activities you plan to implement only count to the extent that they are capable of producing outcomes. Methods are like workhorses. They must be strong and well-suited for the job, and no matter how beautiful they are, the question is whether they can pull the weight.

Unfortunately, grantseekers often allow methods to drive their argument for support. They declare that the problem their organization wishes to address is the "lack of a tutoring program" or "lack of a needle exchange program"—basically, the "lack of" whatever activity they wish to implement. It's a beginner's mistake that sets up a circular, nonsensical argument.

If, for example, you claim the problem is, "There's no tutoring program at the high school," then the outcome you'll probably propose is that "there will be a tutoring program." This argument misses the first step—defining the problem for which a tutoring program is a reasonable response. A rational person's reaction is likely to be, "Why do you think a tutoring program is needed? What problem will it solve?"

To recognize the relevance of the proposed tutoring (the method), funders must understand the challenges and problems the students are facing. Are they at risk of academic failure? Funders must also understand the long-term implications of the situation. How would academic failure harm students' long-term health and well-being? Then, funders need to understand how tutoring could help turn things around. Would the tutoring program result in improved academic performance?

There are three reasons grantseekers make the mistake of arguing for activities rather than for change. First, many people have a hard time differentiating between a problem (the situation motivating action), an outcome (the desired change), and methods (the activities that will produce the desired change). Until you get that straight, you'll be unable to make a coherent argument for grant support.

Second, grantseekers sometimes fail to understand that a grant award is an investment in social change, and funders must be convinced that the change is worth the money. It is always about the change, not the activities.

Third, grantseekers sometimes become so infatuated with the methods they wish to implement that they can't see beyond them—they're smitten. The methods become all-important. The program activities rather than the desired changes become the purpose of the grant request.

Always begin by explaining the situation you are concerned about and why it matters. Then specify the measurable changes you expect to achieve and argue that those changes matter. Only after you've done that are you ready to dive into an explanation of the activities you'll put into place to achieve those changes.

Activities are only a means to an end. That end is results.

Generate Hope

When seeking grants to tackle complex, entrenched problems such as homelessness or poverty, a proposed program may seem tantamount to suggesting that a spoon be used to remove a mountain. Unless you're careful, the crushing weight of negative facts and figures will tinge the proposal with an aura of hopelessness. I call it *the mountain and the spoon* mistake.

One program can't wipe out a complex, entrenched problem, but a coordinated community approach can make a difference.

To move beyond this conundrum, define how your organization's work will contribute to long-term progress. In trainings, grantmaker Kevin Wiberg, a friend and trainer for The Grantsmanship Center, urges applicants to,

"Be sure the proposal speaks to the promise of the work."

There are three main strategies for chipping away at complicated, deep-rooted problems:

Target causes your organization can influence. To be effective, a program must strike at the root causes of the problem, and complicated problems have lots of roots. For example, many factors contribute to homelessness—poverty, substance abuse, mental illness, domestic violence, lack of affordable housing, joblessness, and more. Sort out the various causes, then lean in to the one that fits your organization's mission and expertise. No single organization can tackle every factor that contributes to homelessness, but each organization can target the causes within its realm of influence.

Take a right-sized bite. Once you've focused the approach to address causes you can realistically influence, you may have to narrow the plan further to fit your organization's capacity. For example, while its mission and expertise might be appropriate to assist school-aged children who are homeless, your organization may not have the capacity to assist all homeless children who live in your city. It may have to confine at least the initial work to one neighborhood or age group.

Identify your circle of friends. Organizations that effectively address complex, multifaceted problems don't operate in isolation. They're usually tied to coalitions or associations of organizations that form working partnerships. When various public and private nonprofits coordinate their effort, there's more muscle, additional expertise, expanded resources, and greater promise of impact. Be sure the grant proposal identifies your partners and your organization's role within the larger picture.

One program can't wipe out a complex, entrenched problem. But a well-considered, tightly-targeted approach that is coordinated with other community efforts can absolutely make a difference. A convincing grant proposal acknowledges the complications, then clearly shows how the expertise and capacity of your organization will contribute to meaningful progress.

People who practice grantsmanship are optimists, not pessimists. Still, they're pragmatic. A powerful grant proposal lays out a realistic path for for moving forward and generates hope.

Evaluate

The demand for weights and measures that prove program effectiveness is here to stay. And the value placed on outcomes (results) as opposed to effort (a.k.a. activities, methods, outputs) is a good thing. After all, the mission of a nonprofit is not to "do things." The mission is to have a positive impact.

The value placed on outcomes is a good thing. The mission is not to "do things" but to have a positive impact.

It's hard to find anyone who disagrees with the importance of measuring impact. The disputes are about what to measure, how to measure it, what metrics matter, how data are interpreted, how data are used, and the funder's role in defining success.

There's no question: to develop a competitive grant proposal you must address each funder's specific demand for data. But your organization may need information beyond what is captured in a funder-driven evaluation plan. Give unto the funder what the funder demands, but don't stop there.

An organization that approaches evaluation as a way to strengthen its work—as an obligation of good management rather than merely a funder requirement—will be much more effective and will also win more grants. After all, two primary messages of every successful grant proposal are, "We can make a difference," and, "A grant to this organization is a solid investment." The clearest way to send those messages is with data that document a track record of results.

Take the driver's seat with data. When planning a program, think deeply about what you will need to know, determine what data are required to compete for the grant, then put an evaluation plan into place that meets not only the needs of the funder but also the needs of your organization and other stakeholders.

Suppose funder-required data to assess the impact of a prison reentry program focus only on how often participants violate conditions of release. That may indeed be crucial, but it won't tell the whole story. You may also want to track decreased drug use, completion of high school, successful employment, and other indicators of improved social functioning that will provide a more complete perspective.

Suppose a funder is only interested in quantitative data—things you can count or measure (a person's weight, percentages of increase or decrease in the crime rate, test scores, etc.). That information will be imperative in measuring specific changes but may not capture other results you care about.

Qualitative data, often called *soft data*, are important as well. Soft data document the experiences and feelings of people. This type of information is often anecdotal and expressed in quotes, stories, or what ethnographers call "thick description." Soft data can shed light on why changes are happening or why they aren't, and on what matters to the people you serve.

Think of evaluation data as a compass you consult regularly to keep your organization's work pointed in the right direction. When you take the lead with data, making sure you get what you need to stay on course, you'll have a stronger program and a stronger organization. You will also be more successful in winning grants.

Ethical Evaluation

Grants professionals are often involved in designing program evaluation plans. Almost every funder requires one, but even if it is not required you should include one if possible. A solid evaluation supports accountability to the funder, to your clients, to collaborators, and to your organization's professional obligations.

To achieve cultural relevance, engage those you will serve in designing the evaluation plan. It builds mutual trust and ensures results will be meaningful.

If you don't have the necessary expertise, you'll probably work with a consultant or a highly experienced staff member to design the evaluation. No matter who leads the team, take responsibility to ensure that the final plan included in the grant proposal is ethical.

Evaluation of community-based services is not generally subject to the same rigorous rules and ethics that govern research programs. Still, every evaluation should incorporate basic ethical standards. Educate yourself on ethics in evaluation and use these considerations as a starting point.

Informed Consent

People have a right to understand the evaluation approach, the data you'll be gathering, what you will do with the data, and the possible benefits and risks involved. The plan should ensure that people have enough information to make an informed decision about consenting to participate.

Consent can be active or passive. Passive consent assumes that people will participate unless they ask to opt out. Active consent requires that people sign a form documenting their willingness to participate. The nature of the evaluation activities will determine which type of consent is appropriate.

Generally, passive consent is appropriate for a quick evaluation activity that does not request sensitive or personal information. For example, if you ask people to complete an anonymous survey about their satisfaction with a service, a consent form is not necessary. But if you ask for sensitive or personal information, or if providing information will require a significant amount of time, active consent is appropriate.

No Coercion

People have the right to opt out of the evaluation and still receive services. They can also refuse to answer certain questions, bow out of some evaluation activities, and withdraw from the evaluation process altogether even if they have previously agreed to participate. In an ethical evaluation people understand what's involved and participate willingly. Withholding services, or threatening to do so, when people don't wish to participate is coercion.

Collection and Use of Data

Each piece of information you collect should contribute substantively to assessing program impact or guiding program improvement. Don't subject those you serve to unnecessary scrutiny or collect and retain information that's not relevant to the work at hand. Once you decide what data you will gather and how you'll use it, stick to the plan.

Participant Protection

Consider each aspect of the evaluation plan from the viewpoint of a worst-case scenario. Is there any way the evaluation approach could result in harm to the participants' mental, physical, social, or economic well-being? Think long term. A video of a heartfelt testimonial to the effectiveness of substance abuse treatment could surface years later in a way that embarrasses the person or derails job prospects.

Cultural Relevance

An evaluation approach that is not in step with the people you serve won't provide useful information, but it will demonstrate disrespect that is likely to permeate the entire program. Cultural considerations reach far beyond race, language, religious beliefs, educational levels, sexual orientation and gender identification, country of origin, and income levels. The life experiences of people in the program will also determine the plan's design. For example, if you will be assisting people who have suffered trauma, some approaches will be more appropriate than others.

The best way to ensure cultural relevance is to engage those you will serve in designing the evaluation plan. Engaging them will build mutual trust and ensure that evaluation results will be meaningful.

Confidentiality

Organizations have an obligation to treat people's information with care and to keep it safe from unauthorized use and abuse, so be sure evaluation plans include well-considered approaches for protecting confidentiality. Will you use only aggregate data when reporting? When collecting and reporting data, will you substitute numbers for names? Will access to information be limited? Will databases be secure to the highest professional standards?

No Bias

It is all too easy for unintended bias to infiltrate a program evaluation. Engaging those you'll serve in designing the evaluation plan will help. Having well-qualified and objective people gather and assess the data will also help. Understanding that some evaluation activities are more susceptible to bias than others will guide you to take necessary precautions. For example, recording test scores is in and of itself an objective activity, but facilitating and documenting a focus group is not. Be vigilant against unacknowledged or unrecognized prejudices that could taint perceptions.

Data Integrity

The process of gathering, recording, and storing data should ensure confidentiality, accuracy, and security. Be certain the process of data analysis is appropriate and will result in truthful reports that correctly reflect the successes and challenges of the program.

You will find a plethora of articles and books on evaluation ethics, and you'll find generous people who will share their knowledge. Absorb all you can, and if you are new to evaluation design, seek guidance from an expert to make sure you're on track.

Conducting ethical evaluations is an essential aspect of organizational integrity.

Sustain Impact, Not Activities

Grants are investments in change and funders want to know that the results of grant-funded work will continue beyond the period of their financial support.

Shift your focus toward ongoing results.

In grant proposals, sustainability used to be defined as "the ability to keep program activities going after the grant ends." But because activities only matter if they produce results, we now view sustainability as continuing *impact* rather than continuing activities.

The resources you'll need to sustain impact will depend on the type of changes the program delivers. Programs that change systems (strengthen antipollution laws, make access to higher education more equitable, etc.) can promise ongoing results without the need for ongoing funding. A project that upgrades equipment (improves technology, replaces a heating system, etc.) won't require a great deal of cash to support ongoing maintenance and a long-range replacement plan. But for other types of programs, sustaining impact often means continuing some or even all program activities.

Changing the focus from ongoing activities to ongoing impact will affect your initial program planning. It will guide you to target the root causes of the problem and work toward fundamental change that will continue beyond the grant. It will encourage you to incorporate vigorous collaborations and embed the work deeply into the community so there will be more hands on deck to keep the changes alive. It will instruct you to include sustainability work in someone's job description to ensure it gets the attention it requires from the beginning.

When focusing on sustained impact, think broadly. It's possible that the program you maintain will look quite different from the original. You may find ways to continue some activities without a continuing investment of cash. You may drop or alter activities that aren't producing results. You may scale back activities that are especially costly. Parts of the program may be adopted by other organizations. By sharing the load, you may be able to make the whole thing work with less cash and more community engagement.

Focusing on continuing results also reinforces the importance of an evaluation that produces high-quality data. If you can't document results, why should organizations and individuals in the community help you continue the work? If you don't know which activities are producing results and which aren't, how can you develop a sustainability plan that makes sense?

Occasionally, organizations must respond to a catastrophe or confront a need that is so critical and urgent that ignoring it amounts to ethical neglect. In those cases, you may ask a funder to join you in doing the right thing even if there is no long-term game plan. In those situations, adhere to the philosophy of John Wesley, the English clergyman and founder of Methodism, who counseled: "Do all the good you can. By all the means you can. In all the ways you can. In all the places you can. At all the times you can. To all the people you can. As long as ever you can."

Wesley's philosophy should be used only rarely as an argument for grant funding. Yes, in cases of emergency we may all need to jump on deck to keep the ship afloat, even if its destination is uncertain. But to facilitate real, lasting change in society, we must put our heads together and figure out a plan that will address problems in a sustainable way.

When planning programs, engaging the community, and talking with funders, turn the focus toward sustainable impact.

Teams Are Best

A solid grant proposal is based on planning that translates the concerns of the intended beneficiaries, the community, the applicant organization, and the funder into a clear, rational blueprint for action. Because balancing these various perspectives isn't easy, you may be tempted to go it alone. Don't. As Norton Kiritz said, "Effective planning can't be done in a vacuum, sitting alone in a corner, separate from the views of others."*

As Norton Kiritz said, "Effective planning can't be done in a vacuum, sitting alone in a corner, separate from the views of others."

The best program plans are produced by teams that include beneficiaries, program staff

Grantsmanship: Program Planning & Proposal Writing, The Grantsmanship Center, 2015.

members, collaborating organizations, and other community partners concerned about the issue you need to tackle.

When the planning is done, you also need a team to develop the grant proposal. Even if you draft the narrative yourself and put together most of the supporting documentation, reach out to colleagues for support and feedback.

Program-level staff members can ensure the narrative is accurate and tell you whether the timeline is doable. Finance staff members can make sure you don't over- or underestimate expenses, leave out line items, or fail to adequately address indirect costs. Human resources specialists can make sure the budget reflects salary and fringe benefit policies. Staff members who aren't familiar with the plan can read a draft and point out spots they find confusing.

If top administrators aren't on the team, keep them informed each step of the way. After all, they'll serve as your liaison with the board of directors, communicate with funders, give final approval to the budget, and sign off on submission of the application.

If you try to go it alone, your programs won't be as effective, your proposals won't be as successful, and even though you may win some grant awards, you'll most likely be a flash in the pan that burns out quickly. Go for impact, not personal glory. Go for the long haul, not the quick, feel-good fix. The world needs durable, dedicated contributors, not showboats.

Best Practice Versus Innovation

The nonprofit community is rife with idealists cooking up audacious solutions to stubborn problems. It's a Petri dish, bubbling with notions that just might work. Grants can be a powerful mechanism for supporting innovation, but finding grant support for new, experimental approaches isn't easy.

Nonprofits must:

- **be experts in their field**
- **know when new approaches are needed**
- **offer up good ideas**

Grantmakers must:

- **be open to innovation**
- **be willing to take risks**

The allure of best practices, proven approaches, research-based approaches, and the like is understandable. Funders want their dollars to produce results, after all. But if grantmakers limit their investments to proven approaches, how will nonprofits develop promising innovations, find keys to unlock closed doors, and move the field forward?

Like most conundrums, the solution is to strike a balance, and grantseekers and funders will have to walk the tightrope together. Nonprofits must be experts in their field, know when new approaches are required, and offer up good ideas. Grantmakers must be willing to take reasonable, well-considered risks. Both must honor the good that exists while also moving forward into the promise of what could be.

When working to bring a new idea to life, assess the situation thoroughly. You can't ignore proven approaches. Instead, consider how the new option fits within those approaches, or fills a hole in them, or builds on them. Do some research to see if others have tried something similar and whether it was successful. Connect with those innovators to learn about their work and tell them what you have in mind. Collaborate.

Once you have your concepts and information organized, bring the idea to top administrators in your organization and explain why it has value. Get a green light for action, then reach out to people and organizations who should care about what you're doing. Engage them and build momentum for the work.

Whenever possible, take the new approach out for a test drive. There may be a low-resource way to try out the idea. Perhaps it's a good fit for one of your organization's current programs and can be integrated into that work. Keep detailed notes on implementation, challenges, successes, and outcomes. Promising data from small-scale pilots can be powerful in convincing grantmakers to partner with you to expand the test to a larger scale.

Since you want to engage grantmakers as partners in the new undertaking, start by telling them what you envision and why it's important. Some funders may join you in the endeavor by making grants, some may introduce you to other grantmakers, and some will simply appreciate being informed.

To innovate effectively, understand the field and how the new approach fits within what has already been proven to work. Lay a solid foundation of community support. Be clear in your understanding of the need for the fresh approach and relentless in your advocacy to bring it to life.

Ethics

Each year, grant proposals bring in billions of dollars from private and government sources, and anywhere you find big dollars, you find a significant risk for unethical dealings. To stay clean, organizations need systems to protect against bad behavior. And if you are personally responsible for grant applications, you must stay alert.

Anywhere you find big dollars, you find risk for unethical dealings. Stay alert!

The first step is recognizing hot spots where ethics are most likely to be violated. Each organization will have its own weak points and special circumstances that require close scrutiny. Assess those within your particular environment. Here is where ethical issues most frequently surface:

Finances. Although financial operations tend to get close, ongoing scrutiny, this is still the epicenter of risk. You need to know that the grant requests you submit have accurate, defensible budgets and that promised matching funds are available and committed. You need to know that your organization allocates grant expenditures correctly, draws down grant funds appropriately, and produces accurate, timely reports. You must be confident that grant funds are spent for the purposes intended.

Data Integrity. Competitive grant proposals must include data that support the need for the program and show the success of the applicant agency. It takes time, knowledge, and skill to track, compile, and report data accurately. And sometimes, when good data sources aren't available, it takes even more time to pull together surveys, hold community meetings, or conduct interviews to find out what you need to know.

Given the demand for data, the fact that it is sometimes scarce, and the pressure to meet deadlines, it's all too easy to make up data, citations, and quotes–clearly an expedient but entirely unethical response to the situation. If you are responsible for the proposal, review the final draft carefully and verify data sources. Submitting fake data and then receiving a grant award based on that information is fraud.

Plagiarism. For a good definition of plagiarism, see plagiarism.org. To summarize: it's unethical and illegal to pretend someone else's words or ideas are yours, fail to give credit for words or ideas you've copied or borrowed, or fail to use quotation marks for quotes or provide correct citations. When preparing grant proposals, be careful to cite sources fully and accurately.

It takes consistency and dedication to stay on the right path. Put ethical policies and procedures in place, follow them, and stay alert.

Be Sure It's Worth It

Developing grant proposals is usually deadline-driven work. In the best-case scenario, farsighted, proactive planning will give you a solid program plan with which to work. But even then, you're likely to find yourself with a complicated set of guidelines within which you must articulate that plan. You'll have to gather required attachments and documentation and squeeze everything into limited page or character counts while the deadline barrels toward you like a fast-moving train.

Even when you work for an outstanding organization, the work will be stressful. It's the nature of the job.

In the worst-case scenario, a funding opportunity will emerge that is perfect for a known community need, but no planning will have taken place, no data will have been gathered, no partnerships will be in place, and the deadline will be less than two months away.

While the first scenario is definitely better, both are likely to find you working nights and weekends, and the latter is likely to find you sleeping in your office with your toothbrush in the top desk drawer.

If you turn out a high number of proposals each year, or if you sometimes work on several proposals at once, the vise tightens. I once developed two huge federal proposals at once, and it took a month for me to recover. If you don't have a strong team with whom to work, the vise tightens further. Who wants to be alone at the office on a Saturday? And if administrators don't understand the pressures of your job, you're likely to feel that your sacrifices are unappreciated.

Working for a nonprofit that is overly dependent on grant funding drastically increases the stress. In these organizations, grants come and go, so staff members come and go, and no one wants to lose a job. Overhead expenses stay steady or increase while grant funding vacillates. I knew one grants professional whose desk sat directly opposite the financial manager and who was subjected to a constant stream of sighs and expletives when it was time to balance the books. In these organizations, anxious eyes watch your every move.

You can relieve some of the strain by being relentlessly proactive in every aspect of your job. It's also a great help to work for an organization in which administrators and board members understand the rightful role of grants and don't expect you to single-handedly fund the organization's work. Having a strong team and dedicated community collaborators lightens the load, because going it alone is a proven recipe for burnout.

But even when you work for an outstanding organization that has a sophisticated understanding of grants, the work will be stressful. It's the nature of the job. So be sure that you truly care about the issue you are fighting for. Once, when I'd been locked in my office for days finishing a complicated proposal, staff members slipped pictures under my door—pictures of the beautiful children they helped each day. Those pictures lifted my spirits and reinvigorated my determination.

When you work at an exemplary organization with a mission that aligns with your passion, your role as a grants professional offers you the privilege of making a positive difference in something you care about. Your work will light fires that keep burning and change things for the better. Look for a professional home in which your work will provide deep, personal satisfaction that will stay with you for a lifetime, and bring lasting benefits to the community you care about.

Grantsmanship in a Nutshell

Grantsmanship is a philosophy, a code of ethics, and a set of skills that, when practiced together, can produce positive change. Here is how The Grantsmanship Center defines it:

When you practice grantsmanship:

- You never lose sight of your organization's mission.
- You know your field and stay up to date on relevant research and best practices.
- You know the people and the community your organization serves and treat them with genuine respect, encouraging their input and involvement.
- You're committed to planning because you know it's essential to making a real difference.

- You engage others in planning—staff, constituents, board members, community members, other organizations—because you value diverse perspectives.
- You build partnerships with colleague organizations, not because the funders say you have to, but because you're committed to the expanded viewpoints, resources, and program effectiveness that genuine partnerships bring.
- You view funders as partners, allies, advisors, and advocates.
- You proactively search for funding opportunities that fit your organization's mission and priorities rather than passively waiting for something "right" to come along.
- You refuse to misrepresent or fabricate information, disparage other organizations, or compromise a program in order to win a grant.

A grant is not about money alone, because money by itself doesn't protect battered families, help children to read, fill the plates of the hungry, clean polluted lakes, or open museum doors. But when a grant is used to finance a well-planned program run by a capable and committed organization, it can be a powerful catalyst for change. A grant is a tool—a means to an end.

Similarly, the size of a grant is not the measure of success. A large grant to support an ill-conceived program can be a waste of money. A small grant to support a well-designed program can be tremendously effective. Grantsmanship is not about chasing dollars—it's about getting good results.

Excerpted from "What is Grantsmanship" in *Grantsmanship: Program Planning & Proposal Writing* by Norton Kiritz and Barbara Floersch, edited by Cathleen Kiritz (The Grantsmanship Center, 2015).

Embrace the Power of the Work

Those of us who practice grantsmanship don't need the star-power of a celebrity or the pocketbook of a billionaire to bring about change. Done right, proposal development is a mighty tool that amplifies our influence through the never-failing power of authentic partnerships. Together, grants professionals, community members, organizations, and grantmakers figure out the why of a situation, then hammer out plans to make things better—plans that shout *"why not!"*

For such dynamic work, it's interesting that most people fall into it by accident. I've never met anyone who emerged from college with the dream of writing grant proposals. Typically, a necessity arises within a nonprofit, a proposal must be prepared, the director looks around and there you stand. "You can think, you can write, you're tenacious as a bulldog, and you're stubborn as a stump," says the director. "Want to write grant applications?"

When you step into a proposal development job, you step onto a rollercoaster—a looping track of breathless highs and screaming lows. Winning is as intoxicating as loosing is blistering. Wins bring all sorts of benefits to your community. Losses mean community members who need help won't get it, or that people now getting assistance will soon lose it, and maybe that colleagues will lose jobs.

Activism takes many forms, but when you're slugging it out with 60 pages of application guidelines on a weekend, you're unlikely to think of what you are doing as working for social change. Please know it is. Buried in the mountains of details and fine print is the possibility of making something better. You may be up to your elbows in unintelligible federal forms, spreadsheets that are misbehaving, and the litter of fast food takeout boxes. You may be stressed and cranky. But you are there still, time after time. Why?

You are not there because of the extravagant salary doled out by your organization. You are not there because you can't find another job. You are not there because you are a masochist. You are there because you are committed to the mission. You are hopeful. You believe things can be improved and wrongs can be made right. You care about the people and issues you're fighting for and, darn it, you are too tenacious to quit. You will win some and lose some, but you will always try. You will never give up.

My great hope is that you will embrace the power of your work and understand it as an essential element in the social change toolkit. You are so much more than writers of applications or fillers of forms. You are activists bringing your passions and skills to the battles you choose. You are tough, your work is honorable, and your causes are noble. You help communities dream of something better, then you coalesce the energy and resources necessary to turn the dreams into reality.

Everyone has something they can contribute toward building a better, more equitable society. Those with thundering influence can use it. Those with unfathomable amounts of money can give it. Most of us don't fall into those categories, but when we all bring what we have to offer and work together we can face down the dragons and build up the systems to support change for the better. All of our contributions matter. Everyone can offer time, commitment, and kindness. We can all stand up for or against something. We can take a knee or give a salute. We can vote. And people who develop grant proposals can keep a righteous focus on the mission and do the work right.

If we all offer what we can, and do the best we can, for as long as we can, contributions grand and modest, loud and quiet, public and personal will grow from a trickle into a stream, from a stream into a river, and from a river, finally, into an ocean from which a better world can be born.

Acknowledgments

I am deeply appreciative of the support of The Grantsmanship Center and Cathleen Kiritz, and of the mentoring provided by the founder of the field, Norton Kiritz.

• • •

Because this book reflects the teaching and writing I have done for The Grantsmanship Center since 2000, some phrases are closely similar to the Center's copyrighted material.

The Grantsmanship Center has granted permission for use of phrases that are closely similar to its copyrighted material and of the following specific material:

"The Mountain & The Spoon Mistake" Floersch, Barbara. The Grantsmanship Center Blog, February 27, 2017.

"Lack of a Program Is Not a Grant Proposal Argument" Floersch, Barbara. *The NonProfit Times*, December 18, 2018.

"What is Grantsmanship" in *Grantsmanship: Program Planning & Proposal Writing*. Kiritz, Norton, Floersch, Barbara. Edited by Cathleen Kiritz. Los Angeles, CA, The Grantsmanship Center, 2015.

Barbara Floersch has over 40 years' experience managing nonprofits, writing grant proposals, and administering grants. She has raised millions of dollars in grant funding, served as a reviewer for federal grant competitions, and testified before Congress on reauthorization of the National Endowment for the Arts. Serving as a trainer for The Grantsmanship Center and as the Center's Chief of Training and Curriculum, Floersch developed numerous educational programs and trained thousands of nonprofit staff members throughout the US and internationally. She has published hundreds of articles, contributed regularly to *The NonProfit Times*, and authored *Grantsmanship: Program Planning and Proposal Writing*, the updated, expanded edition of Norton Kiritz's seminal work in the field. Visit her website BarbaraFloersch.com.

Also Available from Rootstock Publishing:

The Atomic Bomb on My Back
Taniguchi Sumiteru

Blue Desert
Celia Jeffries

China in Another Time: A Personal Story
Claire Malcolm Lintilhac

Fly with A Murder of Crows: A Memoir
Tuvia Feldman

The Inland Sea: A Mystery
Sam Clark

Junkyard at No Town
J.C. Myers

The Language of Liberty:
A Citizen's Vocabulary
Edwin C. Hagenstein

The Lost Grip: Poems
Eva Zimet

Lucy Dancer
Story and Illustrations by Eva Zimet

Nobody Hitchhikes Anymore
Ed Griffin-Nolan

Preaching Happiness:
Creating a Just and Joyful World
Ginny Sassaman

Red Scare in the Green Mountains:
Vermont in the McCarthy Era
1946-1960
Rick Winston

Safe as Lightning: Poems
Scudder H. Parker

Street of Storytellers
Doug Wilhelm

Tales of Bialystok: A Jewish Journey
from Czarist Russia to America
Charles Zachariah Goldberg

To the Man in the Red Suit: Poems
Christina Fulton

Uncivil Liberties: A Novel
Bernie Lambek

The Violin Family
Melissa Perley;
Illustrated by Fiona Lee Maclean

Wave of the Day: Collected Poems
Mary Elizabeth Winn

Whole Worlds Could Pass Away:
Collected Stories
Rickey Gard Diamond

Printed in the USA
CPSIA information can be obtained
at www.ICGtesting.com
LVHW040431070824
787522LV00003B/347